Blood Stains

The Lyrics Of Jaysen True Blood

2000-2011, Book 12

By Jaysen True Blood

Notes

Let the party begin. Yes, I have begun to get into the 'feel good' lyrics that party hearty. Though I am not much of a party animal, I did write a few songs for a party atmosphere. Most were to cheer myself up...or simply for the fun of it.

Ridin' High Into The Sun and *Hear The Roar* are influenced heavily by the band *Molly Hatchet* while others hint at hidden secrets. Or a love for the road and performing for crowds. *Remember My Name* puts forth the question we all ask those we love at some point. *The Circle Has Been Broken, Mean It When You Say It,* and *True Believer* address faith and the ever present hypocrisy of established religion. *Dangerous Toys* and *What Have We Done?* Are once again indicative of my rebellious protestor instincts while *Bits-N-Pieces* was named after an Omaha band that had caught my attention in high school...but ended up having nothing whatsoever to do with them.

Long Hot Summer, Pullin' The Curtains Open, and *Another Face From My Past* deal with depression and the realization that nothing is forever. *No One Here By That Name* was a warning to my first wife not to attempt to look for me while *The Lady Won't Let Go* was a thinly disguised expose on my first and second wives' secret...secrets I found out *after* the fact.

For the most part, this collection is an eclectic mix of upbeat and dark as well as the fun and the thoughtful. The mix fits well. Or, at least, I feel they do. They mirror a time in my life when I was stretching my creative wings and trying new things. But it was also a time of deep introspection and realizing my mortality.

~ Jaysen True Blood, 2019 ~

Contents

Free Sample

Verse
I never had the chance to ask
How you were doing these days
Did you take on the task
Of going and changing your ways
Or was all I heard
Just a bunch of lies?

(interlude)

Verse
I didn't catch your reply
Could you repeat it for me?
In the past all you did was a lie
To that we could all agree
Your word was never good
Just didn't sound like it should.

(solo)

Verse
I can't understand a word
You won't look me in the eye
Yeh your words are a bit slurred
Making me think you're telling me a lie
The time you've had was ample
And I just can't spare another free sample.
Oh no.

(solo out)

Only Just Beginning

Verse

Wake up in a cold sweat
The darkness surrounds you
Your sheets are all wet
Is there someone outside your door?
Did you just imagine it all
Or were those steps you heard coming across your floor?
What about those eyes you see along your wall?

Chorus

Your nightmare is only just beginning
Yeh it's only just beginning

Verse

Curled up in a corner of your bed
Paranoid delusions fill your head
You think the world's out to get you
You don't have a single clue
What's real, what's an illusion
What's the deal? What's your solution?
Are you going to turn on your light
Or will you take flight?
(chorus)
(solo)

Verse

You turn on the light
Ready for a fight
Look around, nobody's there
No trace can be found anywhere

What will you do?
Is your hell really through
Or are they all waiting for you
To turn out the lights?
(chorus)
(solo out)

No More Singin' The Blues

<u>*Verse*</u>

The skies may be gray
Yeh it may be raining
I've put my slide away
Ain't been complaining
Yeh I hope happy days
Are here to stay

<u>*Chorus*</u>

No more singin' the blues
I'm lookin' at brighter days
I've found my way through
My depression and the music still plays
That much is true
And there's no more singin' the blues

<u>*Verse*</u>

The days may be hard
And the nights seem long
I may be a lonely bard
Ain't nothing wrong
Because it ain't that hard
To sing my song
(chorus)
(solo)

<u>*Verse*</u>

The world may turn
And life may go on
There's still much to learn

So many battles to be won
Yeh so many bridges left to burn
Before the past is gone
And still I yearn...
(chorus)
(solo out)

Last Call (For A Good Time)

<u>*Verse*</u>

It's twelve o'clock
And all is well
You can hear the band
Clear down the block
And the liquor we sell
Has been in high demand
And it's almost time to close our stand

<u>*Chorus*</u>

Last call for a good time
Better get what you can
One more chance to make it rhyme
Yeh that's the plan
Because this is the last call for a good time.

<u>*Verse*</u>

It's getting kind of late
And we're getting tired
You can have some more fun
Just don't hesitate
Because in here, that's all that is required
Yeh it's another case of hit and run
But don't jump the gun
(chorus)
(solo)

<u>*Verse*</u>

When morning comes round
And we've run out of booze

Yeh when the first light of dawn
Comes on. We'll be outbound
Setting our control on cruise
And we'll be gone
Yeh we'll be gone
(chorus)
(solo out)

Lost And Found

(intro solo)

Verse

Mr. DJ can't you give me
Just a little airtime
Man I'm beggin' ya
Won't you please just agree
Ah just listen to my rhyme
And I'll leave heah.
(interlude)
Mr. DJ give me a minute
Let me explain to you
Just what I want
No I ain't through yet
You know I'm tellin' you the truth
No need to taunt
Oh no, no, no!
(music change)

Verse

Don't make me wait
In the lost and found
Don't seal my fate
Without listening to my sound
I don't wanna stay second rate
I wanna be heavenbound
(solo)
(music change back)

Verse

Mr. DJ won't you play my song
Give it half a chance
I'm sure it'll go far
No there ain't nothing wrong
I won't back down, won't give up my independence
No won't get in my car
And drive away...so play it now!
(music change)
(bridge)
(solo out)

No Slowin' Down

Verse

From now on
The blues are gone
No, no one really won
The battle, on no
And there's nothing left to show
No, nothing left to prove
Now that I'm on the move

Chorus

There's no slowin' down
No time to feel like a clown
It's time to turn that frown
Into a smile
And lay down our arms for a while
Don't let go, don't look back
Because there's no slowin' down

Verse

From here, right now
We'll figure out how
We can change our course
With the help of an unseen force
And with that light that glows
We'll watch as our love grows
And we'll see which way it goes
(chorus)
(solo)

Verse

As time goes by
We'll watch the birds fly
And I'll listen to you sigh
Happily as we grow in love
I'll call you my little dove
You'll call me dear
And you'll have nothing to fear
(chorus)
(solo out)

Mean It When You Say It

(intro solo)

Verse

You never practice what you preach
You're so two-faced
You shouldn't try to teach
That which your views are based
Because your life ain't even close
To your ever changing ideal
And your views' overstatement is a gross
Exaggeration of your own faults
And it's your own soul they steal

Chorus

Mean it when you say it
Don't say the same old bull shit
In your raging fit
Practice what you preach
Happiness is within your reach
Don't become a leech
Sucking everyone dry
Of emotion with your little lie
Because one day, you'll wake up bitter asking why
You have been left all alone
Left to moan and groan
Because you didn't mean it
When you said it
(solo)

Verse

You refuse to be or do
What you expect of others,it's true
And you find that your bitterness grew
Now you're faced with an ugly choice
But in your fear you've lost your voice
What'll they sow now
As you take your final bow?
So as you drink of the bitter brew
What will you do?
(chorus)
(solo out)

Ridin' High Into The Sun

Verse

The dust's risin'
Into the cloudless sky
Reachin' out to the sun
Those who follow me
Will ride for days not realizin'
Askin' themselves why
I chose to run
Rather than waitin' to see
Chorus
I'm ridin' high
Into the sun
Dust risin' to the sky
Because I'm on the run
Verse
Killed a man
Back in Abilene
Who thought he was quick
With a six gun
Now there's a posse with a plan
With Sheriff Greene
Who think they're slick
Chasin' me out of fun
(chorus)
Verse
Left town fast
Never wanted trouble

I found myself in
And now I'm on the run
Don't know how long freedom will last
But I know the reward is double
Guess I can't win
So I ride into the setting sun
(chorus)
(solo)
Verse
I'm goin' home
Ridin' fast as I can
To be with my friends
And the woman I love
Didn't want to roam
Wanted to be a man
And when this road ends
I hope I will be with my little dove
(chorus)
(solo out)

Don't Stop Me

Verse

I'm a man on a mission
No time to make a decision
I've broken my chains
Now only the music remains
No more living a lie
I've got to spread my wings and fly

Chorus

Don't stop me
I gotta be free
Can't you see
This is the way
It's got to be?
So don't stop me

Verse

I've left the past
The future's comin' on fast
No time to stand by
I can't make any more excuses why
No more hiding behind illusions
I've got to stand firm
It's the only solution.
(chorus)

Verse

I'm finally free
No time to give the third degree
I've done my time

For someone else's crime
Now I've gotta let go
Let the music flow
No more holdin' back
This is all we lacked
(chorus)
(solo)
Verse
I've broken my chains
Now only the memory remains
I've found the life I knew
Started my life anew
No time left for the lie
I've gotta move on
Gotta look my future in the eye
(chorus)
(solo out)

One More Day

Verse

I tried every trick
I could find
Added another brick
To the wall I hide behind
I stood tall
Where others fell short
And took the fall
When the judge held court
Chorus
Now all I ask
Is for one more day
Don't give me the task
Because I don't know my way
Verse
I played the game
By their enigmatic rules
I took the blame
When they looked like fools
I wrote the rhyme
That had no reason
And took the blame for the crime
When they committed treason
(chorus)
Verse
I went out of my way
To make things right

They begged me to stay
And finish their fight
I walked the line
Hoping to find love
And I drank their bitter wine
When push turned to shove
(chorus)
(solo)
Verse
I left it all behind
So I could breathe easy
I returned when I found justice was blind
And their music became sleazy
I took up the load
I had left behind
And I hit the road
When they proved to be unkind
(chorus)
(solo out)

Let Go

Chorus

 Sing with me for a while
 Let's give it a little style
 Yeh it's time for the show
 So just let go, yeh let go

Verse

 Nine PM and the place is packed
 Yeh this is what I lacked
 There's a line growing outside
 Waiting to get on the ride
 Last night seemed a little slow
 But tonight I watched the crowd grow
 (chorus)

Verse

 Business is starting to pick up
 Yeh things are starting to look up
 People are buying drinks, they're having fun
 No need to jump the gun
 Yeh time to have a good time
 And listen to the rhyme
 (chorus)
 (solo)

Verse

 It's time to rock
 Yeh rock around the clock
 No time to stop now
 Wouldn't want to anyhow

So let's go on with the show
Yeh let this feeling grow
(chorus) (solo out)

We're Goin' Wild

Verse

C'mon people
We're having a party
And you're all invited
The moon is full
And the music's free
And the bartenders are delighted
That the place is divided
Yeh listen to me

Chorus

The joint is jumpin'
The backbeat's pumpin'
The backdoor girls are bumpin'
And we're goin' wild
Oh yeh
We're goin' wild

Verse

C'mon people
The night's still young
And the fun's just started
The music's turned up
The venue's not quite full
And the love gun's set on stun
'Nuff said
So just fill my cup
(chorus)

Verse

C'mon people
Feel the music's pull
We're not going to stop
Until the sun comes up
Yeh we're sure you'll have a good time
We're going to take you to the top
So take a drink from the good time lovin' cup
And drift away with the rhyme
(chorus)
Verse
C'mon people
Have a good time
Because tomorrow's around the corner
And tonight's got some life
Dance beneath the full moon
And listen to the rhyme
Because the night's going to be a blur
Yeh and there ain't no strife
(chorus)
(solo)
Verse
C'mon people
The booze is flowing free
Yeh and the smoke's so thick
You can cut it with a knife
Yeh and you can feel the music's pull
Don't you see
This ain't no trick
Because we love life
(chorus)

(solo out)

One Man Show

Verse

Up here all alone
I alone play the instruments
One and all
Hear as the organ groans
And the guitar whispers torments
As the curtain begins to fall
Chorus
I am, always will be
The one man show
I set the music free
Always shall the fires glow
For all to see
Let your horror grow
For I am the one man show
Verse
No tricks to ply my trade
I trust no one, it's true
Thus my fortune is made
And as the crowd comes to
I shall sink my blade
Deeper into you
(chorus)
Verse
As I leave
You'll beg for more
One more tale shall I weave

Not telling what fate holds in store
Nor will I grieve
No bitter words, that's what I swore
(chorus)
(solo)
Verse
Ah pretty little succubus
Why do you tempt me?
I was the one with whom
You placed your trust
Now I must set you free
From your jewel encrusted tomb
(chorus)
(solo out)

Headed For A Fall

Verse

Someday you'll understand
All I tried to do for you
I was yours to command
My love for you was true
But you didn't want it to last
No you only wanted to have yourself a blast

Chorus

Now you're going to take a fall
Now your back's to the wall
Yeh you're headed for a fall

Verse

Someday you'll realize
Everything they've told you
Was just one big lie
Yeh and all I ever said was true
But you didn't understand
That love was something you couldn't command
(chorus)
(solo)

Verse

Someday you'll know
That I was there for you
Yeh my love for you was more than just a show
And you'll know it was true
Yeh and just one night
Won't make things right.

(chorus)
(solo out)

Hear The Roar

Chorus

Hear the roar
As we ride into town
On our horses of steel
Shakin' you to the core
Makin' you feel like a clown
Yeh it feels all too real
When you hear the roar

Verse

When it's sundown
We come riding hard
Metal men on horses of steel
No sanctuary can be found
We hold the wild card
Yeh, death is all too real
(chorus)

Verse

Tin badges on our vests
Six guns at our side
Men of metal, nerves of steel
We're the best in the west
Coming down from a wild ride
This time is all too real
(chorus)

Verse

All guns blazing
Retribution's in the air

Like thunder crashing
Dying eyes start glazing
Realizing life ain't fair
When the lightning starts flashing
(chorus)
(solo)
Verse
As the sun goes down
We rise into the sun
Metal men on horses of steel
To another lawless town
Yeh we live by the gun
And the cards of death are what we deal
(chorus)
(solo out)

Louder Than Thunder

Verse

Light the fuse
Watch it burn
Pay your dues
As you yearn
You're free to choose
Which way you'll turn
But what'll you lose
In the cheap day return?
Chorus
Sound the alarm
It's a call to arms
Comin' in loud and clear
The battle is near
And the sounds grow louder
Louder than thunder
Verse
Run for your life
Hear the screams
As they rise above the strife
Is it what it seems?
The end is coming at the end of a knife
And the pool of blood gleams
No more thoughts of your wife
No more hopes or dreams
(chorus)
Verse

Silence in the dark
Rest for a time
Have you made your mark
On the wall you climb?
Did you see the spark
Of hope die in the grime?
Was it just a lark
Or was it your final rhyme?
(chorus)
(solo)
Verse
As darkness falls
Are you truly free?
Has the world got you by the balls
Or can you see?
Are you still crashing into walls
Or is it just me?
As you wait, time seems to crawl
Wouldn't you agree?
(chorus)
(solo out)

Long Hot Summer

Lead

It's gonna be
A long hot summer
(music starts)

Verse

It's been a cold wet winter
Here in my heart
No love could enter
No love could take your place
And make me even start
To lose the memory of your fate

Chorus

It's gonna be a long hot summer
Once again
There's a hole in my heart
Where you shoulda been
Yeh I gave you my number
But you never call
And this burnin' pain has started
To make me feel small
Yeh and it's gonna be
A long hot summer
Won't you set me free?

Verse

It's been a gray wet autumn
Here in my life
No love could make my heart

Beat like a drum
Don't need no more strife
Yeh I've had more than enough
Right from the start
(chorus)
(solo)
Verse
It's been a long dry spring
Here in my life
Could just one call bring
You back to be my wife?
What would you say?
What could have driven you away?
(chorus)
(solo out)

A Trick Of Lights

Verse

Flick of the switch
And everything you know
Is no longer what it seems
It fades away with a twitch
With the afterglow
And with all of your dreams

Chorus

It's all just
A trick of lights
Yeh it's all just
A trick of lights

Verse

With a pull of the shade
It all blows away
Like dust in the wind
Wouldn't have stayed
Wouldn't have remained anyway
As fate grinned
(chorus)
(solo)

Verse

With the sunrise
Comes a new day's course
Filled with challenge
That trip the wise
Without any remorse

As it continues on its binge
(chorus)
(solo out)

An Angel Without Wings

Verse

Baby, baby don't you know
You, you're special to me
And sometimes, sometimes it shows
And sets us both free

Chorus

You're an angel without wings
Baby you know you are
Your love ain't got no strings
Yeh you're my evening star
Because you're an angel to me
An angel without wings

Verse

Baby, baby don't you see
You, you're the only one
And it, it's good to be
Right beside you when I'm not gone
(chorus)
(solo)

Verse

Baby, baby don't you ever run
You, you mean too much
You oughta be havin' your fun
And usin' your magic touch
To bring back the warmth of the sun
(chorus)
(solo out)

Remember My Name

Verse

After I'm dead and gone
After it's all said and done
Will I still be the one
Who bought you the sun
When there was nothing but clouds?
Tell me, did I make it fun?
Didn't I save you from the crowds?
Chorus
Tell me
Will you remember my name
When you're free
To return to the game?
Verse
After my time runs its course
And my life reaches its end
Will I still be your driving force
Will I still be the wind
That filled your sails and brought you to port?
Tell me, isn't it my love I'll send
With you to those distant shores?
(chorus)
(solo)
Verse
After my days are through
And I'm no longer there
Will your love for me still be true?

Will you have fond memories to share
With those you hold dear?
Will I be the one that you
Use to chase away the tears?
(chorus)
(solo out)

Shame On Me

Verse

I broke a few hearts
I played the tease
That's where my crime starts
No I never aimed to please
Chorus
Well shame on me
I was a little too free
It's the way I wanted to be
Yeh shame on me
Verse
I played hard to get
I made money, I had fame
My course had been set
No I couldn't feel the shame
(chorus)
Verse
I showed no fear
I always won the game
My sights were set, my vision so clear
But all my excuses seemed so lame
(chorus)
(solo)
Verse
I broke all the rules
I did things my way
I made girls feel like fools

When I started to play
(chorus) (solo out)

Suddenly Sexy

Verse

She's got moves
That sends chills
Racing down my back
She's got grooves
Yeh she thrills
And it keeps me on track
Chorus
She's suddenly sexy
Yeh she's suddenly sexy
Verse
She's got ways
That makes me cry
Beg and plead
She always plays
Makes me wonder why
She gives me what I need
(chorus)
(solo)
Verse
She's got things
The others don't
And she's all mine
Luck's what she brings
That's what others won't
And she's so fine
(chorus)

(solo out)

The Circle Has Been Broken

(intro- chorus to 'Let The Circle Be Unbroken')
(guitar)
Verse
Your religious views
They're so untrue
This illusion
Is no solution
You've become a dissident
Thinking your knowledge is infinite
You are right
But you're so wrong
You can't win your fight
So sing your swansong
Chorus
The circle has been broken
By your own desire
The words have been spoken
That'll set the world on fire
Your faith is a token
Of your twisted desire
Because the circle has been broken
Verse
Your Mahapralaya
Will never help ya
Your religious vanity
Only leads to insanity
You've led the rebellion

In the name of the sun
Your unholy pride
Makes you choose a side
You followed where they led
And now you've fled
From the truth
(chorus)
(solo)
Verse
Your visions twist to fit
Your lamp remains unlit
Your policy is a lie
Full of the tears you cry
You run to a fantasy
In time to see
That you chase one of two dreams
That ain't what it seems
And now you cry
And you don't know why
(chorus)
(solo out)

Love, Louisiana Style

(Cajun dance hall/Zydeco infused rock)

Verse
Oh ma cherie
Gonna give you love, you'll see
Your man, that's what I'm gonna be
Yeh I'm gonna set you free
Oooooooo-eeeeeee

Chorus
Gonna give you love
Louisiana style
Gonna set you free, my dove
In a little while
Yeh gonna give you love
Louisiana style

Verse
Oh ma petite
Gonna give you a lovin' treat
For you my heart beats
In the middle, that's where we meet
Oh ma amie
(chorus)
(solo)

Verse
Pretty Cajun queen
Don't be so mean
Tell me where you've been
Oh don't make a scene

Why ya so mean?
(chorus)
(solo out)

Dangerous Toys

Verse

The generals have their
Tanks on the ground
And their planes in the air
To war they've been bound
Their battles have been unfair

Chorus

Dangerous toys
For dangerous boys
That's what we have
Because war doesn't
Bring any joy
At all

Verse

The punks in the street
With their guns blazin' away
Killin' anyone they meet
And those caught in the fray
End life under a linen sheet
(chorus)
(solo)

Verse

The peacemakers, they fall
Prey to the angry masses
They're strung up in front of all
To see hypocrisy as it is
But onward they crawl

Cryin' death to all
(chorus)
(solo out)

South Of The Border

(mariachi infused rock/metal)

Verse
Headin' south to Mexico
Where the desert plants grow
Gonna let the tequila flow
In the afterglow
It's time to go
Chorus
South of the border
Yes, everything's in order
To go south of the border
Verse
Headin' to Guadalajara
Gonna find me a pretty senorita
Whose name is Juanita
Who'll teach me how to play the maracas
As I sip pina coladas
(chorus)
Verse
Yeh I'm a hungry little gingo
Who can speak the lingo
Yeh I'm gonna mingle
Act like I'm single
Can't ya hear the bells as they jingle?
(chorus)
(solo)
Verse

Gonna go to Mexico City
Gonna find a senorita who's pretty
Don't ya know it's a pity
I can't get to the nitty gritty
But I'm gonna have a hot night in the city
Oh yeh
(chorus)
Rock it now!
(solo)
Oh yeh!
(solo)
Take it out now!
(solo out)

Take Me To Paradise

(intro solo)

Verse

Baby won't you stay the night
Wrap your arms around me
And just hold me tight
Please set me free
I don't wanna see
The morning's light
I don't wanna be
Left to fight
Wouldn't you agree
Lovin' you is better than taking flight?

Chorus

Take me to paradise
Turn up the heat
Make it twice as nice
Your love is sticky sweet
Yeh it melts the ice
So won't you
Take me to paradise?

(solo)

Verse

Baby won't you set me on fire?
I wanna be wrapped up in you
I love walking your wire
Baby it's true
Don't call me a liar

Don't say we're through
Just take me to the highest spire
No I don't wanna be blue
Make this bed our funeral pyre
And let this storm brew
(chorus)
(solo out)

Come Home

(intro solo)

Verse

It's been seven long years
Since I left home
Through all my tears
I still roam
Searching for something to chase away my fears

Chorus

I hear the voices
[Can you hear what they say?]
I see my choices
[Is tomorrow a new day?]
They seem to say
[What do they say?]
Come home, son
Come home to stay
(solo)

Verse

It's been hard for me
To stand and fight
It would've been easier to be
Someone who just might
Set themselves free
(chorus)
(solo out)

The Lady Won't Let Go

Verse

She's a real smooth operator
Sells lust at the five and dime
She's a real cash separator
She'll take it all over time

Chorus

The lady won't let go
She just wants to see
How much money you'll blow
As she gives you everything
In a single nightly peepshow

Verse

She's the woman of your dreams
But at a higher price
Is she everything she seems?
Or is she just another vice?
(chorus)

Verse

She's a lady of the night
Her office is the street
She's a real beautiful sight
To the men she'll meet
(chorus)

Verse

She's a real luxury
To those who have money
She's in no hurry

Because she thinks it's funny
(chorus)
(solo)
Verse
She's on the loose
She owns the night
Yeh she'll tighten the noose
And make it feel right
(chorus)
Verse
She's not the love of your life
That's not her game
She's not your loving wife
And you're the one to blame
(chorus)
(solo out)

No One Here By That Name

Don't try to find out
Where I live
There ain't no doubt
That they won't give
You what you want

There ain't no one
Here by that name

Don't ask where I'm going
You'll never find me
My path keeps growing
I've been set free
From the chains that held me
(chorus)
(solo)

Don't try following me
You'll never keep up
No you'll never see
Where I am so give up
And just let me be
(chorus)
(solo out)

True Believer

Verse

I never believed the lies
That tempted, it's true
My voice was never among those whose cries
Never made it through
Chorus
I am a true believer
Not a deceiver
Nor a griever
Verse
I never believed anyone
Who said the end was near
I knew they had gone
Under in their fear
(chorus)
Verse
I never believed the deception
That had blinded the rest
I knew it was a misconception
And the truth would always be best
(chorus)
(solo)
Verse
I was never convinced
By what they had to say
No I was never taken in
Because I stood in their way

(chorus)
(solo out)

What Have We Done?

Verse

Look at our lands
We've poisoned them with chemicals
Stripped it of its bands
And its preventative walls
We've polluted our sky
With carcinogens
And all we can ask is why
We're running out of oxygen

Chorus

What have we done?
Where is the sun?
Why does the sky
Always cry
Tears of acid
Making lakes so placid
Go stagnate?
What can we do
Before it's too late?

Verse

Look at our lives
We abuse our health
We ignore our wives
And when discontent creeps in under stealth
We neglect our children
And when we see trouble
We feel the fear then

Watching as the cauldron bubbles
(chorus)
(solo)
Verse
We make fun of dreams
Sayin' they'll never make it
Yeh we claim they're just schemes
Something that just doesn't fit
We try to make others do
The things we think they should
Oh yes, it's sad but true
We did just because we could
(chorus)
(solo out)

Forever Yours

(intro solo)

Verse

Darling, I will never leave your side
I never wanna hurt you
Yeh I know you've cried
When the others were untrue
But I'm not that way
I'll always love you
More and more every day.

Chorus

[Forever yours]
I will be
[Forever yours]
I'll set you free
Because I will always be
[Forever yours]
Forever yours
(solo)

Verse

Baby I never wanna break your heart
I never wanna see you cry
Yeh I've loved you from the start
And that's the reason why
I'll never leave you alone
Yeh I wanna help you fly
Can't you see how our love's grown?
(chorus)

(solo out)

The Ragman

Verse

Baby let me be
The one you run to
To set you free
Yeh when you want a love that's true
Let me be your man
I'll never let you down
Yeh I'll be your biggest fan
And I'll be your little clown

Chorus

I'm the ragman
I'm your number one fan
Baby, I love you
I'll always be true
Because I'm the ragman
Yeh the ragman
(solo)

Verse

Baby let me give
You everything you need
That helps you live
Yeh let's plant the seed
Yeh let me be the one to show
You how love goes
Yeh let our love go
Let it go with the flow
(chorus)

(solo out)

Pullin' The Curtains Open

Verse

Gonna chase away these clouds
Yeh I'm gonna find the sun
Gonna get away from these crowds
And when I'm done
I'm gonna have some fun

Chorus

I'm pullin' the curtains open
Yeh I've been hopin'
To find a ray
Of hope someday

Verse

Gonna chase away this rain
Yeh and find a way to shine
Gonna get these thoughts out of my brain
Yeh I'm gonna draw the line
Or I'll go insane
(chorus)

Verse

Gonna go to Jamaica
Yeh gonna take a holiday
I really wanna take ya
Yeh gonna find a place to stay
And sip a pina colada
All day ...oh yeh
(chorus)
(solo)

<u>*Verse*</u>
Gonna make you feel good
Gonna really go wild
Gonna treat you like I should
So what do you want, child?
Do you want me to do
What I said I would?
(chorus)
(solo out)

Another Face From My Past

Verse

Another memory is lost
Time slips by so fast
But at what cost?
Is the first still the last?

Chorus

It's just another
Face from my past

Verse

The screen goes blank
Words don't mean a thing
Feel like I'm walking the plank
As I look for something
(chorus)
(solo)

Verse

The amnesia grows
The change is good
I'm stuck in the afterglow
Just like I thought I would
(chorus)
(solo out)

Who Was And Who Will Never Be

Verse

You think you know me
You think you understand
What you think you see
Yeh you think I'm just a man
But I ain't what I seem to be

Chorus

Thoughts of who was
And who will never be
All I see
Memories of who was
And who will never be

Verse

You think you can tell me
What I should do
You just can't let things be
That much is true
But you can't break free
(chorus)
(solo)

Verse

You still haven't learned
If you play with fire
You're gonna get burned
Yeh you're such a liar
Yeh everything you got, you've earned
(chorus)

(solo out)

Climbin' The Walls

Verse

Stuck inside this empty room
Nothing really left to do
But to stare into the gloom
Yeh I think it's true
I'm gonna come unglued
If someone doesn't save me soon

Verse

I'll be climbin' the walls
Ain't had no phone calls
Can't stand any more as silence falls
Yeh time seems to stall
As I'm climbin' the walls

Verse

Four blank walls stare back at me
As I pace the floor
When I run and see
Who's at the door
There ain't nobody there
And I don't think it's fair
(chorus)
(solo)

Verse

Time keeps goin' on by
As I sit and wonder
If I can fly
Yes the heart grows fonder

When you wonder why
And the days, they all just get longer
(chorus)
(solo out)

Bits - N - Pieces

Verse

Chippin' away at the wall that surrounds you
What will I find?
Sortin' out the lies from what is true
What really hides inside your mind?
Breakin' down the braces
What will I see?
How many things hide in the spaces?
What will I set free?

Chorus

Bits 'n pieces
That's all I see
Bits 'n pieces
It's all that might be
Left of your humanity
(solo)

Verse

Chippin' away at the ice around your heart
What hides behind it all?
You were a fool right from the start
Now as you take the fall
You wonder where you went wrong
How could that be?
Yeh I wonder how long
It'll take you to see
(chorus)
(solo out)

Rip It

Lead

C-c-c-c-c'mon!

Verse

We got a party goin'
And you're invited
Yeh the crowd is growin'
And you should be excited
So c'mon!

Chorus

Rip it up
Tear it down
Twist it up
And turn it around
(solo)

Verse

We're gonna have fun
All night long
We're gonna ignore the sun
Because a thousand people can't go wrong
So c'mon!
(chorus)
(solo out)